STAR WARS
Life Size

Surprising sizes from a
galaxy far, far away....

Written by
Hannah Dolan

Actual size
BB-8

Welcome!

The *Star Wars* galaxy is filled with fascinating species and droids of all shapes and sizes, but have you ever wondered how big they actually are? This book will show you their real sizes—and you'll be amazed!

Are you taller than R2-D2? Could a porg fit in your pocket? Would you pet a rancor?

Let's find out!

Who's taller?

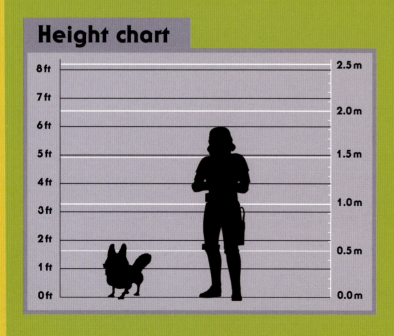

Look out for the height charts in this book. They'll show you how big each character or species is compared to a stormtrooper. How do you measure up to them?

Actual size of **R2-D2's** head.

R2-D2 is a little astromech droid who has seen many big moments in the galaxy, and his photoreceptor captured them all! The circular, black lens works like an eye on his domed head.

R2-D2 rolls around on three legs.

Homeworld: Naboo
Height: 3 ft 7 in (1.09 m)
Weight: 70 lbs (32 kg)

Height chart

Look who just rolled in! **BB-8** is an adorable astromech droid with a round body like a ball. When he feels scared, he scoots away and hides, but he is also very loyal and daring when his friends need him.

BB-8's domed head rolls around on top of his body as he moves.

Actual size **BB-8**

Homeworld: Hosnian Prime

Height: 2 ft 2 in (67 cm)

Weight: 40 lbs (18 kg)

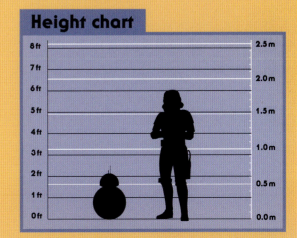

Height chart

Porgs are beakless bird-like creatures that love to be petted and scratched on their heads. They love collecting shiny human objects, too.

Actual size **porg**

Homeworld: Ahch-To
Height: 10 in (26 cm)
Weight: 1 lb (0.5 kg)

Height chart

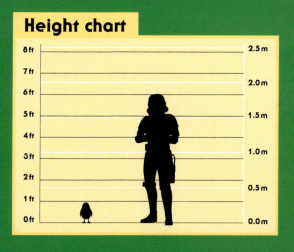

Baby porglets hatch in clifftop nests.

Actual size
porglets

9

Actual size of an **Ewok's** head.

Ewoks might look like friendly furballs, but they're fierce fighters when their homeworld is threatened! They're small but very strong. They live in tribes on the Forest Moon of Endor.

Ewoks craft their own tools and weapons.

Homeworld: Endor
Height: 3 ft 3 in (1 m)
Weight: 66 lbs (30 kg)

Height chart

Actual size of **Chewbacca's** head.

Meet **Chewbacca**, or "Chewie" to his friends. He is a towering Wookiee with silky brown hair all over his body. He is from the forest planet of Kashyyyk.

Chewbacca uses a bowcaster that he built himself.

Homeworld: Kashyyyk
Height: 7 ft 6 in (2.28 m)
Weight: 247 lbs (112 kg)

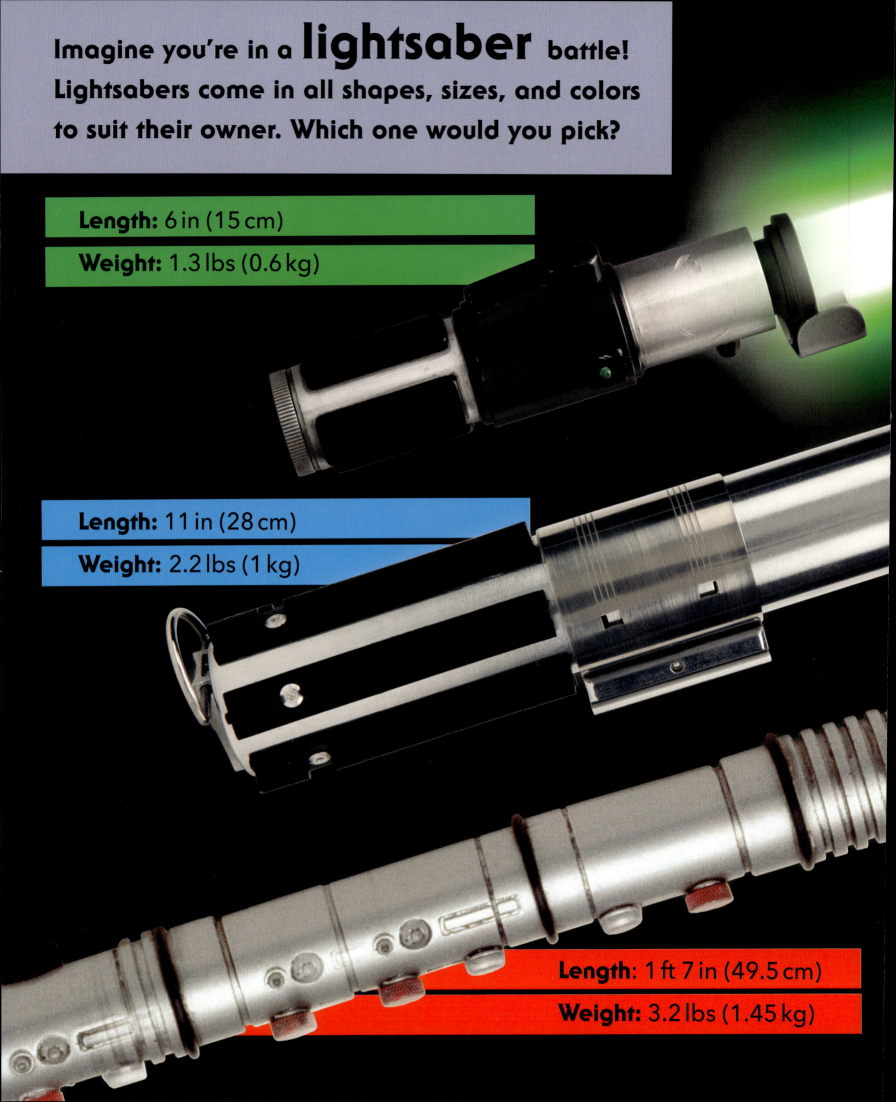

Imagine you're in a **lightsaber** battle! Lightsabers come in all shapes, sizes, and colors to suit their owner. Which one would you pick?

Length: 6 in (15 cm)
Weight: 1.3 lbs (0.6 kg)

Length: 11 in (28 cm)
Weight: 2.2 lbs (1 kg)

Length: 1 ft 7 in (49.5 cm)
Weight: 3.2 lbs (1.45 kg)

Actual size
Yoda's lightsaber

Actual size
Luke Skywalker's lightsaber

Actual size
Darth Maul's lightsaber

This **lightsaber** has two red blades, and it can split into two regular lightsabers.

Actual size of **Darth Vader's** helmet.

Homeworld: Mustafar
Height: 6 ft 8 in (2.02 m)
Weight: 300 lbs (136 kg)

Darth Vader

was once a brave Jedi called Anakin Skywalker but he turned to the dark side of the Force. He needs his black helmet and suit to live, after he was badly injured.

Darth Vader is a cruel, cloaked Sith Lord who wields a red lightsaber.

Height chart

Homeworld: Hoth
Height: 9 ft 10 in (3 m)
Weight: 331 lbs (150 kg)

Wampas create lairs in icy caves.

Blink and you might miss a **wampa** hulking toward you! Their thick, white fur camouflages them on their frozen homeworld. They are massive, fierce predators.

Height chart

Actual size of a **wampa's** head.

With scaly gray skin and bird-like feet, **Lanais** are built for life on a windswept ocean planet. The females take care of the ancient ruins of the first Jedi temple, while the males mostly live out at sea.

Lanais sing and whistle as they do their daily chores.

Homeworld: Ahch-To

Height: 5 ft 1 in (1.55 m)

Weight: 88 lbs (40 kg)

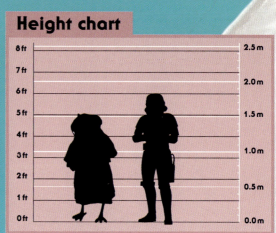

Height chart

Yoda

How do you measure up to Yoda? He might be small, but he is immensely strong in the Force and a huge presence in the galaxy. A wise and powerful Jedi Master, he has trained Jedi for centuries.

As the oldest, wisest Jedi, **Yoda** serves as Grand Master of the Jedi Order.

Homeworld: Not known
Height: 2ft 2in (66 cm)
Weight: 37 lbs (17 kg)

Actual size **Yoda**

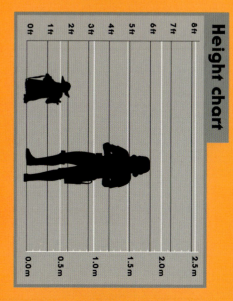

Height chart

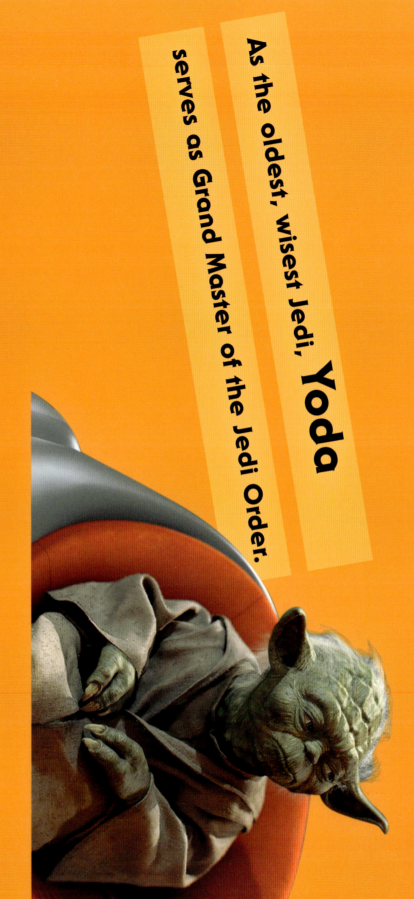

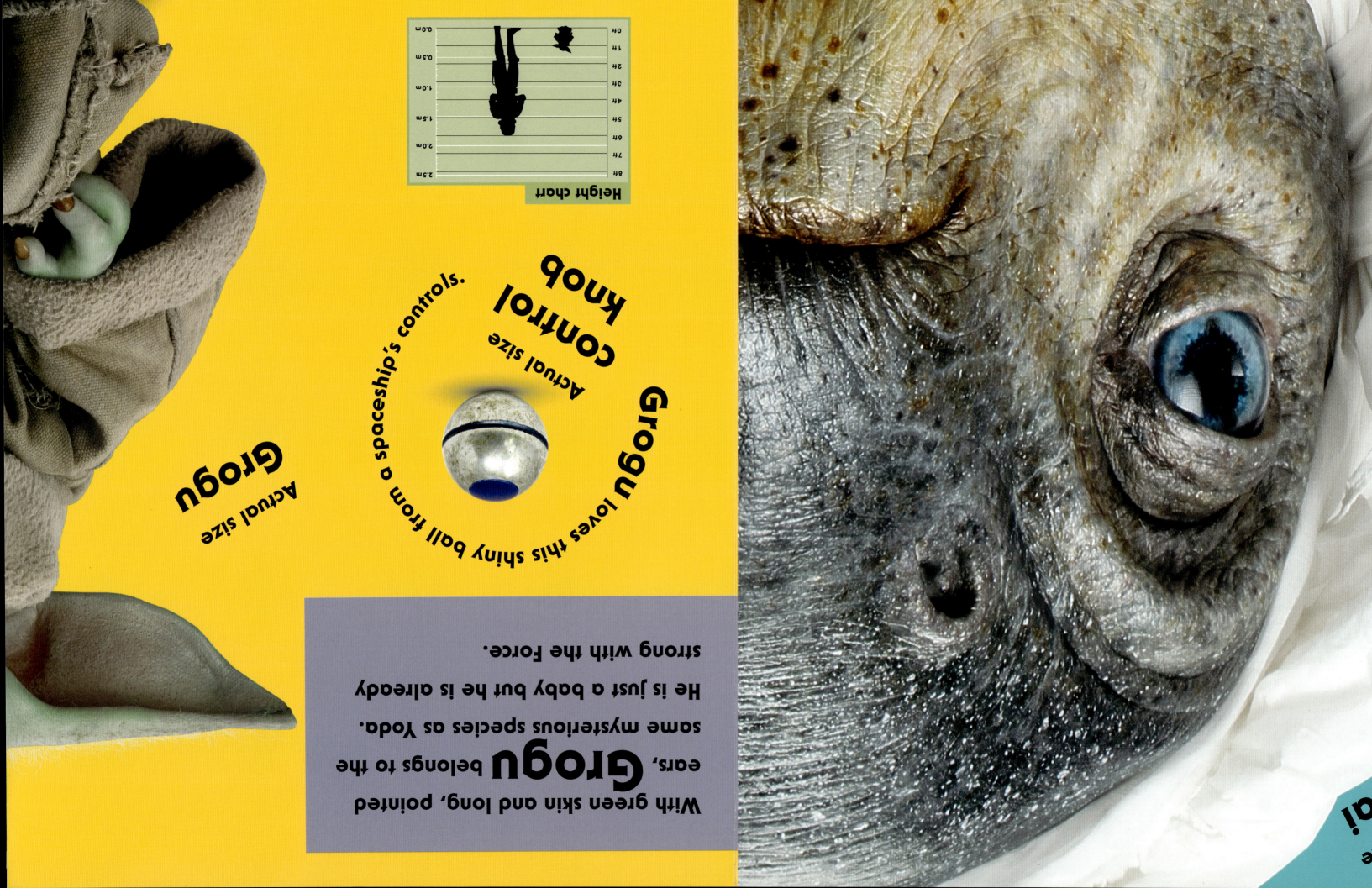

Height chart

Grogu
Actual size

Control knob
Actual size

Grogu loves this shiny ball from a spaceship's controls.

With green skin and long, pointed ears, **Grogu** belongs to the same mysterious species as Yoda. He is just a baby but he is already strong with the Force.

Loth-cats

Furry **Loth-cats** look cute and cuddly, but don't try to stroke one! You have to earn their trust. These feisty felines are excellent hunters, with sharp teeth and claws.

Homeworld: Lothal
Height: 1 ft 9 in (54 cm)
Length: 2 ft 4 in (70 cm)
Weight: 22 lbs (10 kg)

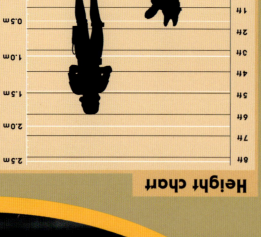
Height chart

Sabine Wren's **Loth-cat**, Murley, loves to take a nap.

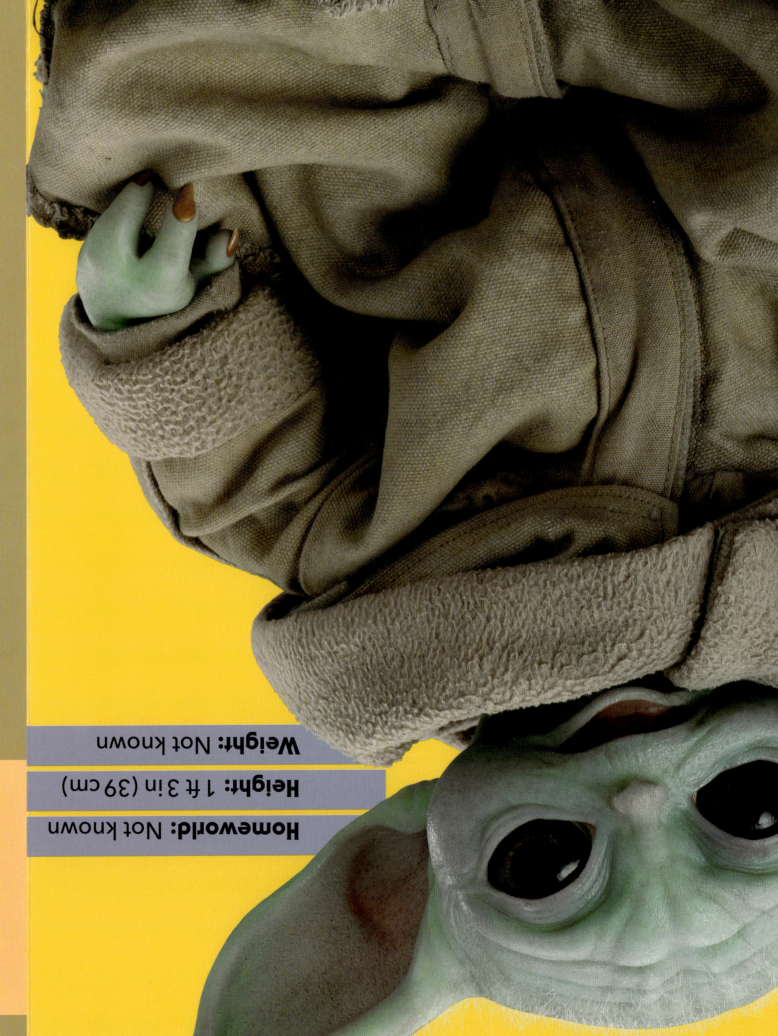

Homeworld: Not known
Height: 1 ft 3 in (39 cm)
Weight: Not known

Actual size
Loth-cat

Pleased to meet you, **C-3PO**! This gold-plated droid always has good manners, but he worries a lot. He has seven million of the galaxy's languages stored inside his memory banks.

Actual size of **C-3PO's** head.

R2-D2 is always by **C-3PO's** side.

Homeworld: Tatooine
Height: 5 ft 9 in (1.77 m)
Weight: 165 lbs (75 kg)

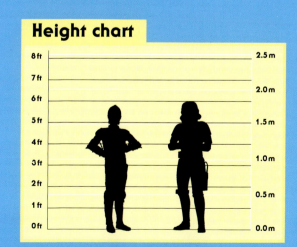

Height chart

Homeworld: Dathomir

Height: 16 ft 5 in (5 m)

Weight: 3,638 lbs (1,650 kg)

Rancors have tough hides and sharp claws.

Actual size of a **rancor's** tooth.

They may have big, toothy jaws, but **rancors** aren't all that vicious—unless they're provoked, then you should run for the hills! They are deadly predators, but they can be tamed in the right hands. Would you dare to try?

Actual size
Kowakian monkey-lizard

Kowakian monkey-lizards

are sometimes kept as pets. The small, floppy-eared creatures like to tell silly jokes, so they're pretty fun to be around.

Salacious B. Crumb is Jabba the Hutt's jester.

Homeworld: Kowak
Height: 1 ft 11 in (58 cm)
Weight: 26 lbs (12 kg)

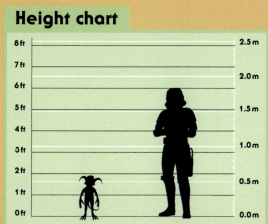

Height chart

You do not want to be eyeball to eyeball with **Jabba the Hutt**. This slithering gangster is one of the shadiest characters in the galaxy. He has a fiery temper and a big appetite, so bring snacks.

Actual size of **Jabba's** eyeball.

Height chart

Live paddy frogs are one of Jabba's favorite snacks.

Homeworld: Tatooine

Height: 5 ft 9 in (1.75 m)

Length: 12 ft 10 in (3.9 m)

Weight: 2,994 lbs (1,358 kg)

Move carefully around **mouse droids** because they are easily startled! These boxy, beeping little droids carry out many simple jobs aboard big starships, whizzing around on four wheels.

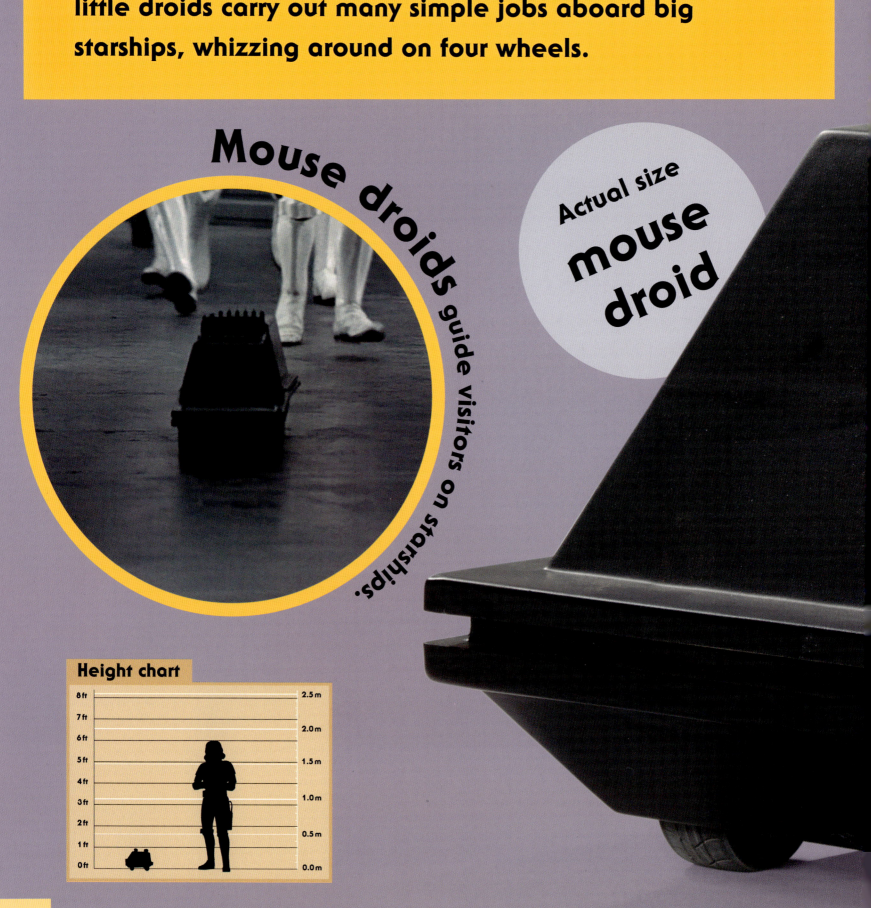

Mouse droids guide visitors on starships.

Actual size **mouse droid**

Height chart

Homeworld: Chad
Height: 10 in (25 cm)
Length: 1 ft 9 in (54 cm)
Weight: 13 lbs (5.9 kg)

Actual size of **Boba Fett's** helmet.

Homeworld: Kamino
Height: 6 ft (1.83 m)
Weight: 172 lbs (78 kg)

This is **Boba Fett**, one of the most feared figures throughout the galaxy. He is a bounty hunter who is paid large sums of money to capture targets for dangerous individuals like Jabba the Hutt.

Boba Fett wears a green and red suit of tough Mandalorian beskar armor.

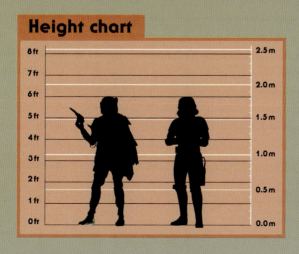

Height chart

Oki-poki don't miss a thing!

These highly sensitive little rodents have big, pointy ears that can hear everything around them. They love to munch on thistlebuzzers.

Oki-poki live in colonies on desert cliffs.

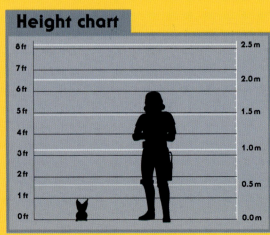

Height chart

Homeworld: Pasaana, Koboh
Height: 1 ft (30 cm)
Weight: 10 lbs (4.5 kg)

Actual size
thistlebuzzer

Actual size
oki-poki

43

You might hear this fox-like creature before you see it. A **vulptex** has white crystals on its fur that make a jingling sound and protect it from predators.

Vulptices live on a planet covered by thick salt.

Homeworld: Crait
Length: 3 ft 11 in (1.2 m)
Weight: 20 lbs (9.1 kg)

Actual size
D-O

Homeworld: Not known
Height: 1 ft 6 in (46 cm)
Weight: 5 lbs (2.3 kg)

D-O is a happy little roller droid who was cobbled together from beaten-up droid parts. He used to be owned by a Sith who treated him badly, but now he helps out his new friends in the Resistance.

D-O really admires his brave droid friend BB-8.

Height chart

Senior Editor David Fentiman
Project Art Editor Jon Hall
Senior Production Editor Jennifer Murray
Senior Production Controller Laura Andrews
Managing Editor Emma Grange
Managing Art Editor Vicky Short
Publisher Paula Regan
Art Director Charlotte Coulais
Managing Director Mark Searle

Packaged for DK by Plum Jam
Editor Hannah Dolan **Designer** Guy Harvey

For Lucasfilm
Senior Editor Brett Rector
Creative Director Michael Siglain
Art Director Troy Alders
Story Group Leland Chee, Pablo Hidalgo, Phil Szostak, and Kate Izquierdo
Asset Management Chris Argyropoulos, Elinor De La Torre, Gabrielle Levenson, and Sarah Williams

First American Edition, 2025
Published in the United States by DK Publishing,
a division of Penguin Random House LLC
1745 Broadway, 20th Floor, New York, NY 10019

Page design copyright © 2025 Dorling Kindersley Limited
25 26 27 28 29 10 9 8 7 6 5 4 3 2 1
001-349384-Jun/2025

© & TM 2025 LUCASFILM LTD.

All rights reserved.
Without limiting the rights under the copyright reserved above, no part of this publication may be reproduced, stored in or introduced into a retrieval system, or transmitted, in any form, or by any means (electronic, mechanical, photocopying, recording, or otherwise), without the prior written permission of the copyright owner.
Published in Great Britain by Dorling Kindersley Limited

ISBN 978-0-5939-6924-3

DK books are available at special discounts when purchased in bulk for sales promotions, premiums, fund-raising, or educational use. For details, contact: DK Publishing Special Markets, 1745 Broadway, 20th Floor, New York, NY 10019

Printed and bound in China

www.dk.com
www.starwars.com

This book was made with Forest Stewardship Council™ certified paper—one small step in DK's commitment to a sustainable future. Learn more at www.dk.com/uk/information/sustainability

Actual size
Jedi training remote